F E N G

SPACE CLEARING

and

PURIFYING

LILLIAN TOO

ELEMENT

Shaftesbury, Dorset•Boston, Massachusetts
•Melbourne, Victoria

© Element Books Limited 1999
Text © Lillian Too 1999

First published in the UK in 1999 by Element Books Limited,
Shaftesbury, Dorset SP7 8BP

Published in the USA in 2000 by Element Books, Inc.
160 North Washington Street, Boston, MA 02114

Published in Australia in 1999 by Element Books
and distributed by Penguin Australia Limited,
487 Maroondah Highway, Ringwood, Victoria 3134

Illustrations Peter Greenwood
Cover design by Design Revolution
Design by Design Revolution
Printed and bound in Hong Kong by Imago

British Library Cataloguing in Publication data available

Library of Congress Cataloging in Publication data available

ISBN 1 86204 608 5

Contents

This book and kit are dedicated with much
love to my Dharma friends and family, and especially
to our precious Dharma master and teacher
the Ven. Lama Zopa Rinpoche.

Introduction

This book is written in response to many requests I have received to clarify the issues of space clearing and purification, which are wonderful adjuncts to the practice of feng shui. They enhance the quality of surrounding energies by causing them to become pure and crystal clear. In my previous books on feng shui I stayed silent on this matter, mainly because I did not wish to introduce a subject that should only be undertaken with sufficient understanding. But as feng shui is gathering so much momentum, it is timely to present this extra dimension to the practice of feng shui.

Clearing the space of negative and stale energies (or chi, see Understanding energy page 14) that build up over time is the vital first stage of purification. Energy becomes excessively yin when there is illness or death. It becomes stale when air is stagnant and fetid and negative when there is anger, quarrelling and fighting. All these energies cause chi to be blocked and they have to be cleared before good sheng chi can be restored.

Purifying the space then builds on the clean energy that is apparent after a clearing exercise. It creates an environment that is pure sheng chi. The air feels soft and very gentle and there is a feeling of lightness and cleanliness. The energies harmonize beautifully and everything stays in balance. For a long time, space purifying was a secret practice known only to masters of the esoteric and it is only recently that many of the ancient rituals involving the use of aromas, incense and sounds have been revealed. Space purifying is best undertaken only after space clearing has been undertaken.

Space clearing

In the old days, space clearing rituals were usually undertaken by Taoist or Buddhist monks who chanted special prayers accompanied by the clashing of cymbals and beating of gongs as well as the burning of incense. These rituals were performed to bless new homes by purging them of negative chi, or to dispel tired energies that cling to residences and disturb new residents. They were also often undertaken before the construction of homes and buildings to assuage and appease the spirit *nagas* (or dragons of the earth). These spirits might be tempted to cause harm to residents occupying the new homes if permission were not first sought from them to occupy the space and land.

The Chinese believe that the spirit of the dragon

permeates the land and that only when his auspicious cosmic breath is tapped can good fortune be enjoyed. It is therefore vital that the earth dragon should never be upset or injured and, indeed, he should be persuaded and bribed with elaborate ceremonials. Blessing rituals thus involved the making of "offerings" like bowls of fruit, cups of wine and water and the burning of candles and incense. In the old days, only monks and feng shui masters were deemed knowledgeable enough to conduct these ceremonies.

Enhancing the cosmic chi of the celestial earth dragon will bring good fortune.

Space purification

In exactly the same way, there were also special purifying rituals that were carried out after a death in the family to cleanse the energies of the home. The rituals balanced the presence of excessive yin energies that had been created by the death. They involved the chanting of prayers and ringing of bells and were often conducted after the funeral ceremonials had been completed.

Each technique involved a cacophony of yang energy-inducing methods. The tools used were lights, incense, and sounds and it was believed that these were the three main intermediaries that could appease the earth dragon. The brightness of lights combined with the fragrance of incense and the sound of chanting were believed to cause the dragon to create massive amounts of sheng chi – the auspicious chi that brought good fortune.

Thus, wealthy families who could afford the services of monks and other experts often arranged space clearing and purifying ceremonies each time they moved into or built a new home. Less well-endowed families usually had to make do with burning three joss sticks to invoke the earth deities to bless their homes.

The start of each lunar New Year was similarly characterized by the firing of crackers that caused loud noises to scare away stale energies and welcome the new. This traditional greeting of the New Year was a more affordable method of clearing the air of any negative energies, and its practice continues today among the more traditional Chinese. Financed by their business communities, Chinatowns around the world also retain this custom to ensure business continues to be good or improves in the New Year.

With today's increased understanding of feng shui comes the ability to perform those same rituals that were performed by the monks of another time and age. We, too, can dissolve and clear our space of bad energies, and purify stale energies, replacing them with clear, crisp, luck-enhancing energies. With the aid of specific tools, massive quantities of sheng chi can be attracted into the home. By using the space clearing and purification rituals described in this book, the energies of your home will become crisp, clean and clear so that sheng chi can flow in in vast quantities.

A burst of firecrackers clears away bad energy instantly and effectively.

The space clearing kit

This book contains specific methods of using sounds, lights and incense for space clearing. Chapter 1 describes the most successful space clearing methods, starting with the simplest and moving on to using such items as rice, salt and feng shui mirrors. Chapters 2 and 3 then develop the ideas of space purification using incense and a singing bowl. It is this last that contains the most advanced methods of space purification.

Burning incense holder

❂ This black ceramic dish is used for holding burning incense as you move around the room clearing the space. The image of the yin-yang symbol on the dish symbolizes the balancing of the energies (see page 38).

Sandalwood incense ingots

❂ These are special and auspicious blocks of incense fashioned to resemble gold ingots. You will only need to purify your space once a month using one of these. Once they are lit, smoke is released and it is this smoke that is used for the purification rituals (see page39).

Kathmandu Valley aroma sticks

❂ These aroma sticks give off a slightly more pungent and intense incense. They are made from a mixture of wild mountain herbs and plants from the Solu Khumbu region of the Himalayas and from the Kathmandu Valley. They are thus especially potent for space clearing (see pages 40–41).

Singing bowl

❂ These wonderful bowls, which have to conform to strict specifications for them to "sing" correctly, are excellent for transforming the chi in your home into auspicious, happy chi. Use them regularly to balance the energies of your home and to awaken your own vital chakras. These are the seven vital points of your body where energy concentrates and evolves.

The singing bowl also introduces yang essence into the heart of your home. Over time, the bowl responds to your own energies, so keep it wrapped up in some soft material (velvet, silk or brocade) and use it regularly so that its music tunes in to the vibrations of your home (see pages 47–49). The singing bowl included in this kit has been made of seven types of metals including gold and silver. There is thus great potential for obtaining a very, very pure sound.

Cushion

❂ It is important to place this small round cushion beneath the singing bowl whenever you carry it around or stand it on a surface. The cushion improves the sound of the bowl, making it purer and allowing it to ring on for longer (see pages 53–55).

Wooden mallet

❂ This small mallet is an integral part of the ritual of the singing bowl. By tapping the bowl three times, the ringing sounds are established from which the vibrations of the room are purified. Also use the wooden mallet to rub the rim of the bowl to create the singing sound, which is like a gentle soothing humming. Take care of your mallet since without it you cannot make your bowl sing (see pages 53–55).

The ritual of space clearing

Improving the quality of energy that surrounds you can be undertaken in many different ways, and each culture of the world has its equivalent of the Chinese method of feng shui clearing and land/building blessing rituals and ceremonies. It is entirely a matter of personal preference what you wish to do. How elaborate the rituals and ceremonials are depends on the individual. Some people are more comfortable with simple, fast methods while others love elaborate ceremonials that involve the burning of fragrant incense accompanied with mantra chanting.

I belong to the latter group of people because I love the rituals of space clearing and purification. I adore using incense and moving around my rooms rubbing my singing bowl and chanting mantras. After each space clearing ritual I feel uplifted and enjoy the crispness of the energy around me. I walk around the rooms of my home savouring the beautiful energy.

I do not keep to a timetable or a specific schedule. But over the years I have developed sensitivity to the energies of my home. I can instantly feel when there is imbalance and disharmony. So I undertake space clearing according to how I feel each day. When I or any member of my family succumb to a cold or to the flu I do my space clearing twice a day to literally "clear the air" of the sick energy.

When to use
space clearing

Space clearing done once a month is sufficient and space purification can perhaps be done twice a year and at least once just before the start of a new year. Having said that, do whatever makes you comfortable.

•

Once you become adept at space clearing and purifying, you will no doubt want to do it as often as I do. For example, each time I travel I always do it the first day I get back as this allows me to re-balance the energies of my sleeping and work places. The more you practise, the more you will develop an acute awareness and sensitivity to the energies around you. This is a skill that develops over time and you will find that you start tuning into the environment in a very special way. Simultaneously, your practice of feng shui is heightened.

•

Here are some other instances of times when you may want to practice your space clearing techniques.

•

❧ If you find that you and your family are going through a spate or period of bad luck when everything seems to be going wrong.

❧ When members of your family succumb to illnesses.

❧ When you move into a new home that you are renting or buying or, say, a new room at college.

❧ When you move to a new office or start a new job.

I also burn incense around the room each time we have a particularly severe argument in the home since this washes away any anger that may be lingering in the air. This makes for better relationships. Over the years it has created greater harmony in the home. There are fewer disagreements. Less flaring of tempers. Less anger.

Understanding energy

Burning joss sticks clears and purifies your living space.

Energy or chi is invisible; it has neither form nor substance, yet it exists and it is powerful. Chi flows in the environment and in your personal space. It is described in the ancient texts of feng shui as the dragon's cosmic breath. This colourful description has been interpreted to refer to the lines of energy that occupy space. It can be negative or positive and it can bring good feelings associated with contentment or it can bring extreme unhappiness. In feng shui terms, energy lines can be friendly or hostile, creating exceptional good fortune and wonderful material well-being. Or they can bring misfortune, loss and even death.

Good chi flows contain balanced yin and yang energies.

Feng shui masters believe that the energies that surround a living space vibrate at different rates; and that these energies can be vibrant and favorable or they can be deadly and ill-fated. In feng shui, this is described as being too yang or too yin. The energy of a space can also be harmonious or disharmonious based on the relative representative element(s) of the space. The ways in which harmony and

balance in energy can be created in the living space is what the practice of feng shui is all about. This book adds the extra dimension of space clearing and purification to dissipate hostile energy and help maintain the balance and harmony of good energy. Feng shui speaks of four types of both auspicious and inauspicious chi.

When the chi is balanced your space will be blessed with the auspicious dragon breath.

Auspicious chi

Auspicious chi is known as *sheng chi* and this type of chi is also the most propitious of the four separate types of the auspicious chis, which bring prosperity, growth, wealth and success. A dose of sheng chi in the vicinity of your main front door attracts luck and fortune to your home, and this happens when the orientations of your door have been designed according to feng shui guidelines.

But to get the most from your feng shui arrangements, this chi should be constantly replenished. It must be allowed to accumulate. It must never be allowed to become stale or to stagnate. When any home is closed up and residents leave it unoccupied for a period of time, chi tends to grow dull, thereby losing its luster and its ability to bring opportunities and good fortune. This is when space clearing becomes important.

Upon re-occupying the home, encourage fresh, new chi to enter by letting the main and other doors stay open for

Replace stale energy by opening windows and doors to allow the fresh chi in.

a while. Also throw open the windows to let the chi flow in and out of rooms. This simple replacement therapy instantly allows fresh new chi into the home, which can be further enhanced by undertaking some of the space clearing techniques given in the following chapter.

In addition to improving the flow of sheng chi, there are other feng shui guidelines that explain how you can similarly welcome three other types of chi. Health chi has to do with longevity and good physical health, and this is known as *tien yi chi*, or the doctor from heaven. When the home has been energized with tien yi orientations for its residents and longevity symbols have been placed in specific corners according to feng shui, regular purification of these energized spaces will keep the chi fresh, effective and potent. The best methods to use for maintaining tien yi chi are those that involve the use of incense and mantras (*see* pages 42–43).

The third type of auspicious chi is *nien yen chi*, which brings harmonious relationships luck for residents. This refers to reliable friendships, to productive relationships with staff and with bosses, to the social life of residents and, most importantly, to maintaining harmony between spouses and siblings. Again, there are specific feng shui methods to create this sort of harmony in the home; once created they are best maintained with regular use of space purification techniques that involve the use of a singing bowl (*see* pages 47–53). When the bowl creates music for the home it also creates wonderful vibrations that ensure there is good chi balance.

The pure vibrations of a singing bowl create auspicious chi.

Finally, there is the chi that enhances the personal development and growth of residents. This chi is known as *fu wei chi*. It is

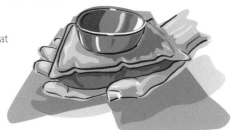

best kept alive and well with regular space enhancement exercises that are also undertaken with the singing bowl. When accompanied with visualization and meditation, the singing bowl creates the most wonderful and pure form of chi, and this chi tremendously enhances personal growth. It will bring forth all that is best in the people residing in such homes.

Inauspicious chi

Inauspicious chi is frequently known as *shar chi* (translated as killing breath), and it is this that causes residents to suffer loss of wealth, good name, descendants, prosperity and happiness. However, shar chi should more correctly be referred to as *chueh ming shar chi*. This type of bad feng shui represents the most harmful killing breath. The other three types of killing energy are described in lyrical terms. The *lui shar chi*, or six killings chi, and the *wu kuei chi*, or five ghosts chi, are also harmful but these bring bad luck of relatively lesser degrees. Finally, there is the hostile chi that brings mild bad luck, and this is known as *ho hai chi*. All four of these types of deadly dragon's breath cause bad feng shui and they can be corrected in a variety of ways.

Bad chi can be temporarily dissolved with space clearing

How to diagnose for bad feng shui and how to correct it is not within the parameters of this book. But bad chi can be temporarily dissolved with the space clearing and purification techniques that are described in the following chapters. In the longer term, though, it is necessary to change orientations, directions and even the placement of doors and furniture to correct bad feng shui. Space clearing techniques alone are usually insufficient to overcome bad feng shui, but they are excellent for maintaining good feng shui brought by the inflow of auspicious chi.

C l e a r i n g
h o s t i l e   s p i r i t s

The techniques contained in this book can be undertaken by anyone. They are excellent for clearing stagnant energies and bringing freshness to a stale environment.

•

But they are ineffective against the presence of wandering, hostile spirits. If you suspect that your house or room is haunted, what you need is a priest or a monk or some holy man who has the expertise and the spiritual knowledge and strength to deal with such phenomena. Feng shui space clearing techniques are not to be seen in the same light as exorcism.

•

Having made this distinction, however, I want to explain that a few of the old feng shui masters like Mr Yap Cheng Hai, my feng shui mentor and great friend, are also very well versed in spiritual knowledge. For instance, Mr Yap prides himself on being something of a "ghost buster".

•

He has an awesome reputation here in Malaysia and he says laughingly, "All ghosts run at the mention of my name!" Indeed, Mr Yap has regaled me with hilarious tales of his experiences with the haunted palaces of India (now converted into hotels), the old vaults and catacombs of Rome (now tourist places of interest) and even talking to the spirits of mummies in the British Museum. Mr Yap is an expert at exorcism but he keeps this practice completely separate from his practice of feng shui.

•

I urge you to do the same. Do not even attempt to play with these spiritual matters. Unless you possess some protection in the form of prayers, mantras or religious amulets, you should never attempt to use the space clearing techniques in this book to offend wandering spirits that may be living in your home. If you wish, however, you can place water and some food as offerings as you move around the home clearing the space, and indeed a preliminary method contained in this book uses salt and rice (see pages 25–26) to cleanse the living space when you first move into a new home. Other than that it would be best if you avoided any kind of confrontation with anything spiritual unless you have a proper teacher to guide you.

CHAPTER ONE

Space clearing rituals

Start by learning how to undertake simple space clearing practices, which you can apply immediately to your personal space. This space is defined as your own room, home or office. Look on these practices as feng shui clearing rituals that are performed with the intention of lightening surrounding energies that have become heavy with excessive imbalance. Try to develop a routine to your space clearing practices so that you will continually freshen those energies that have become stale around you.

Simple space clearing

At its simplest level, space clearing is implicitly undertaken each time you repaint your home, move your furniture around or hang a new picture on the wall. Simple household chores of cleaning, sweeping and airing the cupboards are, of themselves, acts of space clearing that symbolically introduce fresh new energies. They also ensure that the chi of your home never becomes stagnant, stale or dies altogether. Dying chi causes the dissipation of precious yang energy and both luck and health will begin to suffer.

Good feng shui thus has to be maintained, just as do homes. It is important to be constantly aware of the freshness of the chi in the home, and for this reason, a well -kept home that is frequently cleaned, aired and used generally has better feng shui than a home that is allowed to become dirty, cluttered and smelly. Clean and well-kept places rarely suffer from an excess of yin energy, and when properly energized with sounds and lights, there is usually plenty of the precious yang energy so vital for the houses of the living.

I encourage people to vacuum their homes at least once a week, to air their rooms by opening the windows at least

Always use fresh or fake flowers as dried flowers cause excessive yin energy.

once a month, and to regularly open their cupboards and let the stale energy inside escape to be replaced with fresh energy. I frequently remind my readers to throw out dying plants and flowers and never to decorate their homes or offices with dried flowers. Fake ones are definitely better than the dried and dead variety. Once a year it is also a good idea to wash curtains and shampoo carpets. Each of these aspects is an integral part of housekeeping, but they are also good feng shui routines. A well-kept home is infinitely luckier and happier than a home that suffers from neglect. This is, of course, only one aspect of the feng shui perspective, but it is an important part of the practice.

Remember that you can use these simple methods to dissolve all sick and unhealthy energies, as well as to temporarily dissolve inauspicious energies until you can introduce longer-term changes to improve either the orientation of your home or the location of your furniture. Rooms previously occupied by bedridden or sick persons, or in a home that has just had a death in the family, particularly benefit from space clearing rituals.

Starting a space clearing ritual

Before you start, decide which of the many different methods given in this book you wish to use and then gather together all the tools you will need. However, irrespective of the method selected there are some basic ground rules to follow and these are:

- Be clear that what you are doing is space clearing and not space enhancing.
- Think seriously and focus your mind on what you are doing.
- Be very relaxed and understand that you are clearing the energies around you and not praying to or invoking any spirits.
- Undertake all space clearing activities in the morning after the sun has come out. Never undertake space

clearing after the sun sets. Nor should you clear space on an overcast or rainy day. You will always get better results when energized by a dose of precious natural yang energy supplied by the morning sun.

☯ Resist the temptation to perform space clearing rituals for other people. There is an unwritten rule about disturbing the energy of space that does not belong to you unless you possess some protective amulet. Observing this advice will protect you from being inadvertently hurt by hostile spirits that might be present in other people's space and who do not know you. Every space contains the presence of spirits as well as chi. In space clearing, you are addressing only the invisible energy lines that affect your personal well-being.

Fans are symbols of protection against people with bad intentions.

Using fans

In the old days, one effective way of shielding yourself from bad energies was to carry a fan. Ladies usually carried these fans as protection against energies inadvertently met that might prove harmful. For example, suddenly meeting a funeral procession while out walking is considered bad luck and having a fan shields you from the excessive yin energy emanating from the funeral.

Using rice and salt

This is a very popular ritual that is used by authentic masters of feng shui, although each master adds his/her own practice to accompany this clearing technique. It is used when entering a new house for the first time, or when taking over a new office. The ritual involves moving around the external boundaries of the home in a clockwise direction, sprinkling a mixture of raw rice grains and sea salt. Make sure you have sufficient mixture before you start.

● Throw the mixture at the base of the wall and as you do so think,

"The rice is offered as charity to any wandering spirit so all coexist in harmony, and the salt cleanses the space of all negative, sick and hostile energies."

Rice and salt can be used to clear hostile energy.

● After walking around the outside of the home, repeat in the inside, moving from room to room and walking in a clockwise direction around each room. Throw the rice and salt mixture on the floor, at the base of the walls.

● At the front door, throw three handfuls from the inside outwards and then throw three handfuls from the outside inwards. But don't throw too much of the mixture in each handful.

❧ When you have finished, leave the rice and salt on the ground until the next day before cleaning them away. Use a vacuum cleaner rather than a broom for clearing up. The act of sweeping negates what you have done.

Some practitioners use bells and burn joss sticks when they perform this ritual. I sometimes use this rice and salt method in conjunction with the burning of mountain incense method (see pages 40–41).

Using a pagoda

A pagoda is a circular or octagonal building that is usually nine levels high, although sometimes it has only seven levels. In feng shui, this pagoda symbolizes the best and safest place to capture and imprison negative chi. The pagoda was also said to be an effective "prison" for wandering spirits that may do harm to the human race. Some contend that the pagoda is the Chinese version of the Indian Buddhist *stupa*, which in Sanskrit means relic preserver, since stupas are regarded as holy receptacles of the Buddha's relics.

In feng shui, if you hold a symbolic pagoda in your left hand while sprinkling rice and salt with your right hand, it is believed that any wandering spirit with evil or bad intentions will take fright and run. The symbolic power of the pagoda is also invoked when it is incorporated into wind chimes that are meant for pressing down on the bad luck of a particular corner or sector of the home.

Indeed, some five-rod wind chimes are made with several layers of roof levels above the rods to simulate the pagoda. The five rods cause hostile chi to rise up through the hollow tube and be transformed into auspicious chi. The pagoda captures any bad chi that may escape.

Pagodas made of copper or ceramics can be purchased very inexpensively in any Chinese curio shop or supermarket.

Using a feng shui mirror

You can also use a mirror to absorb all the bad and stale energy that may have collected in your home. Select a small circular mirror, about 7.5 cm (3 in) in diameter (you can find such mirrors in a Chinese souvenir shop). Designate it as your feng shui mirror and always use this same mirror. Mirrors used for space clearing should not be used for other purposes. My space-clearing mirror, which I have used for 15 years, is mounted on a crystal and agate frame and it has a silver dragon and phoenix design on its back.

The pagoda is a symbol much feared by bad spirits.

The hand held mirror can be a great personal symbol of protection.

◎ Move around the rooms in the house holding the mirror so that it reflects the walls and every corner. Concentrate in particular on dark corners and places that are seldom used. Be especially thorough with toilets and kitchens.

◎ When you have walked around the whole house, soak the mirror in salt water for a few minutes. This serves to cleanse and dissolve all the bad energy collected in the mirror. The solution should be seven parts water to one part sea salt and the mirror should be soaked in the salt solution for at least three hours. It is best to use water that has been energized by the sun, which means standing it in the sun for at least three hours. The combination of sun and salt is a very purifying combination. After soaking the mirror in this solution, wipe it dry and wrap it in a soft cloth. Keep the mirror inside a drawer or cupboard and do not let it reflect things in a casual manner. Most importantly, do not let it reflect any of the residents in the home as you clear the space in this way.

Using air

A very good clearing ritual incorporates crisp and clear air. The higher you are, the thinner will be the air, but also the cleaner and breezier it will be.

- Once a week, open two windows at a time in your home and invite the air from the outside to enter. Allow it to sail in slowly.

- If you open all the windows at the same time, the air will come in too fast and when that happens it becomes hostile and damaging. Instead, allow the air to flow in slowly and if you can let it meander, so much the better. To achieve this, open one window in one room and another in another room. This creates a suitably gentle flow.

- The best time to do this is at dawn when the energies of the day are pure and crisp. During the summer months, when yang energy is strong, cleaning the energies of your home at sunrise introduces energy that is not too excessively yang. In the winter months you can do it during late morning or early afternoon when the sun gets stronger. While it might seem foolish to bring the cold air into the home, the air actually brings in fresh yang energy that is actually good for it.

Fresh air brings in a dose of new clean energy.

Using sunshine

A variation of the use of breeze and air is the benefits of sunshine for space clearing. Nothing is as effective as sunlight if you want to get rid of stale energies that may have been caused by excessive neglect of the house or simply because a home has not been occupied for a while.

Invite the yang energy of sunshine into your home.

- Open the doors to all the rooms and draw back the curtains to allow the whole house to be filled with sunshine. Remember that sunshine is the greatest source of the precious life force – the yang energy that brings such wonderful good luck.

- On the east side of your home, open the windows to greet the morning sun. On all the windows that face west, hang faceted crystals to catch the strong western sun of the afternoon.

- When you clean your furniture and floors it is a good idea to occasionally use water that has been standing in the sun for at least three hours. This is water that has been energized by the sun.

- If you have a garden, always make sure that trees and plants do not become so dense and overgrown that they completely block out the sun.

Using sounds

The best way to use sound to clear space is with the use of special instruments like bells and cymbals. To complement these sounds, the chanting of mantras also works wonders. Indeed, almost all the religions of the world use a combination of sounds and prayers to bless a space. This is probably because sounds are especially effective in purifying vibrations (see pages 41–43 for more information on chanting mantras).

Little cymbals hit with a wooden mallet are excellent for creating sound.

I have been told by master practitioners that the simple act of clashing cymbals at the entrance to shops and at each corner of a room is sufficient to scare away negative energies. The sharp clanging sound of cymbals also scares away lingering naughty spirits, who prefer to move to quieter areas.

- ❧ If you have a pair of cymbals, clash them three times in front of your main door before moving around your rooms in a clockwise direction and clashing the cymbals three times in each corner.
- ❧ You can do exactly the same with bells made of metals, especially those that have been specially made to produce exquisite sounds. I have discovered that some of the best bells for space clearing can be found in India and Kathmandu. These give off sharp clear

notes when their sides are hit or rubbed with a leather or wood mallet. They are also often adorned with decorative auspicious symbols or the wonderful OM MANI mantra.

❀ Bells are not rung like church bells. Instead, they are best used in space clearing by hitting them with a small wooden mallet like the one provided in this kit. At the front of the main door, beat the rim of the bell lightly three times and focus on the sound created.

Then slowly walk around the living area in a clockwise direction, allowing the sound of the bell to resonate off the walls. At each corner, beat the bell a little harder to create a slightly louder sound.

❀ Continue in this way until you have gone around all the rooms. In the toilets and kitchens, unoccupied rooms and store rooms, beat the bell a little louder than normal. These rooms will benefit hugely from the cleansing, and any lingering stagnant energies will be dissipated.

A metal bell, when hit by a wooden mallet, creates a good sharp, clear sound.

❀ You can do the same thing with metallic bowls. Using a singing bowl is extremely powerful following space clearing so a whole chapter has been devoted to their use in this book (see pages 44–45).

With a bang

If you think you have a severe problem with your living space, an excellent way to clear the negative energy is to let off a string of firecrackers. The use of a loud sound is often very effective in clearing the energy inside the home.

A popular Chinese custom, usually undertaken during the lunar New Year, involves hanging long strings of firecrackers from the highest level of the home down to the ground. The firecrackers are lit from the ground up. These strings of firecrackers can be as long as ten storeys high, and they can take 30 minutes to burn all the way to the top, in the process giving off loud bangs and scattering bits of red paper all around the front entrance. The symbolic meaning is most auspicious since it ensures that the coming year will be cleared of negative and inauspicious circumstances.

The loud burst of sound from firecrackers instantly clears negative energy.

- If you would like to use firecrackers in a similar way, burn a string of them around the front part of your home to get rid of negative energy. But make sure you obtain a permit to do so – and do ask permission from your neighbours!
- To achieve a similar – and safer – effect, I prefer to hang a symbolic firecracker and play loud modern dance music instead. To simulate the burning of red paper in front of my main door, I hang a red cloth with an auspicious design printed on it.

Using lights

Another excellent method of cleansing the energies inside the home, and especially when these energies have become excessively yin, is to use lights. Energy in the home turns yin when there has been a death in the family, particularly when the death has been after a long period of illness.

● After the funeral, wash the room that had previously been occupied by the deceased. Then open all the windows and cupboards and turn on all the lights in the room for three hours. If you like, purchase a string of Christmas lights, place it in a broad-mouthed bowl and also turn on the lights for three hours.

A cluster of candles are an excellent instant remedy for a lack of yang energy.

● Turn on the lights in this way for 49 nights in a row and the room will have been eloquently re-energized with a massive dose of wonderful yang energy. You can use this method in conjunction with the incense methods described in the following chapter (see pages36–41).

● If you prefer, you can also use candles, in which case you should light seven, eight or nine of them. The number 7 is very lucky for this period of 7, which ends in the year 2003, while 8 is a prosperous and auspicious number and 9 represents the fullness of heaven and earth. It is not necessary to use candles that are long lasting. As long as they can burn continuously for three hours each night, it should be sufficient. Please note that in using candles you should never leave an open flame unattended.

● My favourite way of using lights is to use oil lamps since these are clean, efficient and economical. I also like using Christmas lights as they are much less dangerous.

Using fragrances

Finally, there is a growing popularity in the use of fragrances to cleanse the space around us. This is an idea that I can definitely identify with. I do this every day anyway in that I spray water laced with lavender oil in my home. I do this to enhance rather than cleanse my space because I am a great believer in aromatherapy. I believe that fragrances enormously enhance the living space. Lavender oil soothes the mind and brings out the creativity in people.

Each fragrance evokes a different mood and so can be used to achieve a different goal. I recommend the use of scented oils and waters to lighten and enhance the energies around you.

Use the fragrance of herbs and plants to energize and enhance your living space.

CHAPTER TWO

Purifying energy
with incense

The use of incense is one of the most popular methods used by the Chinese to symbolically bless and purify the energies of their homes. Incense purifies the energies and this is not to be confused with space clearing. Feng shui masters usually recommend that you use the methods in the preceding chapter to clear the space first before attempting to purify it.

Space purification enhances the energies that surround you. It creates a good flow of auspicious sheng chi, and when properly done encourages the accumulation of the dragon's cosmic breath. Using incense to undertake space purification is especially effective because it represents the combination of fire with fragrance.

While you can use any kind of incense for space purification, you should always use it in a special incense burner to enable you to burn the incense while moving around the rooms of your home. The smoke that rises from the incense mingles with the energies in the space, thereby purifying it.

The quality of space purification depends on the quality of incense used. The incense used by the Chinese to make joss sticks is excellent for purification purposes and the preferred incense is almost always made from sandalwood or a mixture of sandalwood with another incense. This is a favourite of mine and I burn sandalwood incense almost daily because I like its light fragrance.

Incense from India and Nepal tends to be stronger and more pungent and is usually too heavy for small spaces. Having said this, I would like to point out that incense is a very personal thing. Try a few before settling on the one that you feel pleases you the most. You may like to take a trip to Chinatown to purchase a few packets of incense sticks that are sold either as coiled sticks or as joss sticks. These are relatively cheap unless you specify that you want sandalwood, which is usually a lot more expensive.

Choose an incense and an aroma that you especially like to purify energies in your home.

Space purifying
with incense

Break off a few pieces of coiled or straight incense sticks and
light each piece at one end. Then place them in the specially
designed incense burner supplied in this kit and allow the
smoke to emit it's fragrance strongly.

•

Once you have a nicely burning stack of incense move around each
room in your home or office in a clockwise direction.

•

Walk from room to room making circles with the incense burner
around doors and windows. This multiplies the purification at these
important entry points into your home or office. Pay special
attention to the main front door and to the back door.

•

Also pay special attention to rooms that are important to you such
as your bedroom or workroom. If there are bedrooms where sick
members of the family are convalescing or one that is occupied by
someone who is very ill, spend a few extra minutes here each time
you undertake this incense practice.

•

When you have finished purifying all the rooms, allow the incense to burn itself out. Do not empty the incense ash down the toilet or throw it into a bin. Instead, wrap it in a piece of paper to later empty into the earth in your garden or in a park.

Using incense ingots

If you wish, you might like to use very special and auspicious incense blocks that have been fashioned to resemble gold ingots. Several of these sandalwood blocks are included in this kit. One ingot is usually sufficient for you to move around the entire house and you should only need to purify with such a block once a month.

The ritual is symbolic of actualizing gold inside your home. The Chinese of the Far East and, more especially, the Chinese of Taiwan are particularly fond of burning ingot incense in their homes. Many use these incense ingots for their spiritual and religious practices, too.

❧ To use the ingot, ignite a small portion of the ingot and when you see a fire, lightly fan out the flame but make certain the ingot is simmering red and the incense is burning and emitting smoke.

A fake gold ingot can represent wealth and prosperity.

◑ Let the ingot simmer in this way in your incense burner and move around the rooms of your home in the same manner as described above.

Adding a more powerful incense

Incense purification works best of all when you burn what I call mountain incense made from herbs or small plants that grow in the pure air of very high mountains. My favourite is a mix that contains extremely fragrant incense powder made from pure wild mountain plants from the Solu Khumbu region, near to the base camp of Mount Everest in the Himalayas.

The Solu Khumbu region of the Himalayan mountain range is about 14,000 feet above sea level. This is a very holy part of the Himalayas and it is a region that is much revered by the Buddhists of Nepal, Tibet and the surrounding area. It is believed that the Lotus Buddha, the glorious Padmasambhava, who brought Buddhism to Tibet, hid many of his secret teachings in caves found in this region.

The mountain plants that come from this part of the world are thus considered to be so pure and special that it can be difficult to obtain them. Incense made

Incense made of herbs from the high mountains are the most pure.

with them is only ever available in small quantities and so is expensive. As a result, the aroma sticks provided in this kit contain Himalayan incense mixed with incense from plants that grow around the Kathmandu Valley.

- To use this incense, burn one of the gold ingots in the incense burner as described on page 39 and then sprinkle a tiny bit of the Kathmandu Valley and Himalayan mountain incense mix on top of the burning ingot. It is very fragrant.
- Let the aroma permeate all the rooms of your home. Move in a clockwise direction, as before, and smell the incense as you move around the rooms.

Chanting mantras

If you are familiar with purifying mantras, you can chant your special favorites under your breath as you use the incense to purify rooms. My feng shui mentor, Mr Yap, has told me that this is an excellent way of purifying any home and he always uses them to purify the land and houses whose feng shui is designed or corrected by him. Indeed, the purifying mantra, which is addressed to the Buddha of Boundless Age, is Mr Yap's favourite. He sings this hundred-syllable mantra to the tune of Beethoven's fifth symphony and he sings it very well. Mr Yap is convinced that the same spiritual Being inspired the two – the mantra and the symphony.

The mantras I use are Buddhist prayers transmitted to me in their original Sanskrit. The sounds of these mantras resonate in beautiful balance with the music of the singing bowls, and also with the special ritual bells that can be used instead of the bowls. Such mantras have to be transmitted by high lamas to their students and as such I am unable to put them in this book. However, you may use your own prayers if you so wish to strengthen the feng shui practice of space clearing and purification.

Chanting the OM MANI mantra

Enhance the flow of auspicious chi by burning incense when chanting.

It is an excellent idea to chant a simple mantra as you move around the room with the incense burner. As the smoke rises and spreads around the room, chant the wonderful purifying OM MANI mantra into the smoke so that as the smoke spreads around the room, the mantra symbolically blesses the home.

The OM MANI mantra is a six-syllable mantra that is probably the most famous mantra in the world. It is chanted daily by every Buddhist of the Mahayana tradition, but it is also used by many non-Buddhists who recognize it as a powerful aid for their meditative practices. The mantra is:

OM MANI PEH ME HONE

Buddhists recognize this as the mantra of their Buddha Chenrezig, the Compassionate Buddha, who is called Avalokiteswara in India, the Goddess of Mercy Kuan Yin by the Chinese, and Canon by the Japanese. By whatever name this Buddha is known, this mantra is regarded as being most powerful. Those of you who wish to do so, may chant it 108 times while purifying your home with incense.

After you have finished all the rooms, silently think to yourself:

"I dedicate this purification practice and the chanting of this mantra to the harmony of my home, to the harmonious relationships between the members of my family and to our harmonious relationship with outsiders so that we may all experience continued good health and happiness."

You can also chant this mantra even if you are not Buddhist or you can chant any kind of purification prayer that you know. The use of the mantra is, of course, optional. It is not really a part of feng shui, but I have discovered that incorporating any spiritual aspect to feng shui's space purification adds much to the singular practice of feng shui itself.

CHAPTER THREE

Purifying energy
with the singing bowl

Singing bowls are found in different cultures where sounds feature prominently in their spiritual rituals. Originally brought to the West by "spiritual tourists" and New Age enthusiasts who sought to understand the sound phenomenon in prayers and special ceremonials, today the singing bowl enjoys growing popularity. It is especially efficient for the space purification practices that use the powerful effect of sounds in feng shui.

Singing bowls are usually round and metallic and they are made in different sizes. The quality of the sound is usually determined by the thickness of the rim of the bowl, and the quality of its humming resonance and singing vibrations depends on its depth. The most important characteristic is that when a singing bowl is rubbed, hit or tapped it produces a wonderful pure sound. Even if you just tap the bowl with your fingernail it will send forth a beautiful sound. Singing bowls can be polished or matt and they can be in any metallic shade.

I prefer bowls to bells or cymbals (see pages 31–32) because a container in this crucible shape is such excellent feng shui. These bowls also signify a receptacle waiting to receive good sheng chi luck while simultaneously capturing and trapping all bad energy, transforming it into good energy. The bowl thus serves the dual purpose of feng shui – to counter bad killing shar chi and to contain the auspicious luck bringing sheng chi.

To be authentic and to produce the special singing sound, the bowl should be a round crucible shape. The ratio of the circumference and depth of a singing bowl can vary, but the small bowl included in this kit is fairly thick and round in shape. It comes from the Himalayan region in the Kathmandu Valley of Nepal and, as with all authentic bowls, is made of seven different metals, one of which must be a precious metal such as silver, gold or platinum. The singing

The singing bowl in this kit has been produced to create the purest of sounds.

bowl especially commissioned for this kit is made of tin, copper, zinc, iron, lead, silver and gold.

I asked for a tiny bit of gold to be incorporated into each bowl not just to improve the sound, but also because it symbolizes auspiciousness. Thus this bowl has a golden glow. Using seven types of metals is also traditional as each of the metals represents a planet.

- Gold represents the sun, the ultimate source of yang energy.
- Silver represents the moon, the ultimate source of yin energy. By using silver and gold together, the union of yin and yang is represented inside the bowl.
- Copper represents Venus.
- Iron represents Mars.

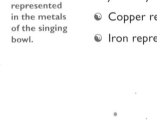

The sun, moon and planets are represented in the metals of the singing bowl.

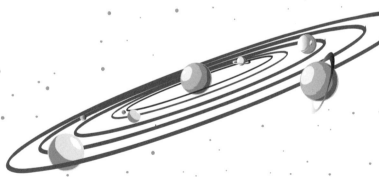

- Tin represents Jupiter.
- Lead represents Saturn.
- Zinc represents Mercury.

The proportion of each metal is a closely guarded secret, and some of the more special bowls use metal alloys that remain a mystery to modern craftsmen. Each of the seven metals produces an individual sound, including harmonics, and when combined the sounds produce the exceptional singing sound that is so effective and easy to use for space purification.

Tuning in to the singing bowl

Before you do anything with your singing bowl, spend some time getting to know it. Every singing bowl has roughly the same sound but there are always slight differences in the balance of sound and harmonics, rendering the sound of each bowl unique. Remember, too, that every space and environment is different and will make the bowl resonate differently. In addition, every person possesses his or her own energies, which also change from moment to moment. The same bowl could well sound different at different times.

Also, note that as your living space becomes purified with regular use, the singing sounds emitted each time will become purer, clearer and sharper to reflect the cleaner energies of the air around you. Develop an awareness of these improvements.

- Let the singing bowl included in this kit sit comfortably on the special cushion on your upturned left palm. Spend a few seconds tuning in to the heaviness of the bowl.

- Then take up the wooden mallet and gently strike the rim of the bowl with it. Each person will hear a different kind of humming, singing sound. Some will hear deep undertones followed by a throbbing sound while others will focus on undulating overtones.

- Strike the bowl again and again to become familiar with the sounds that envelop the room. Allow yourself to enter the sound waves that have been created by lightly closing your eyes. Give yourself free rein to experiment with the way you strike the bowl and you will discover many delightful surprises.

- Alternatively, strike the bowl and after tuning in to the sound, gently but firmly use the wooden mallet to press against the rim of the bowl. Move it around the rim in a clockwise direction, keeping it in contact with the bowl. You will start to hear the bowl singing as it absorbs the energy in the atmosphere, and as you move the mallet slowly around the rim, this singing becomes a vibration. Once you succeed in making this singing sound, walk around the room to let the humming purify the energy.

Over time, you will become familiar with the bowl and be able to feel the vibrations of its sounds. Eventually, through the tones and undulating vibrations, you will be able to detect the initial disharmonies that after a small period of time, become more harmonious. The sound of the bowl itself starts to balance the energies around it, and once the energies become balanced, the singing bowl sings melodiously. It converts all the wonderful auspicious chi around the home into a delightful humming that soothes and calms.

Get to know your singing bowl and make it sing for you.

The importance of sound in feng shui

It is believed that sound is produced by all beings and by all things, even those that are inanimate and have no life, like structures, mountains and hills. All things emit energies and have their own sounds, but this sound changes, depending on the quality of energies around it at any given moment.

•

Scientifically, this is explained by the phenomenon that all things are a collection of atoms that dance and produce sounds by their movements. When the atoms are in harmony, the sounds produced are pure and melodious. It is said that in the beginning, the wind created everything on earth and atoms danced ceaselessly producing songs that were both creative and auspicious, as well as sounds that were destructive, causing disintegration.

•

Sound can thus be used to soothe the energies of the atoms in any living space, causing them to become balanced and harmonious. As such, the use of sounding objects is a very ancient practice in all the countries of Asia. Temple bells, drums, gongs and other instruments in addition to bowls were often used in space blessing and other rituals.

•

The Chinese emperors often kept special ringing stones in their possession, supposedly for luck. They also adorned their bodies with jade stones that are said to produce a ringing sound when hit together.

The benefits of singing bowl purification

The singing bowl can:

- ☯ enhance the energies of the living space
- ☯ transform inauspicious energies into auspicious energies
- ☯ activate the element energies of particular corners.

In addition, many people feel uplifted after a space has been bathed with the harmonics and tones of a singing bowl. Sometimes, the sounds even instil feelings of profound peace. The explanation is that the humming harmonics of the bowl creates ultrasonic sound waves that internally massage the human psyche thereby evoking a feeling of relaxed well-being. Externally, it massages the vibrations and wavelengths of the living space, thereby creating the harmony so necessary for attracting auspicious good fortune.

When to use the singing bowl

Singing bowl purification can be done as often as you like. The simple method of producing the special humming sounds of the singing around the room not only attracts the good fortune sheng chi, it also opens the chakras of the human body (see page 11). So when you undertake this practice, focus your mind and concentrate clearly on what you are doing. Space purification of this kind is simple but immensely effective in creating a very calming influence. If you are new to this practice, my advice is to do it once every ten days.

I usually use singing bowl therapy only after purifying my space with incense. My home will have then been filled with precious yang energy that is pure and balanced, especially when I have used my special mountain incense. Then, when I use the singing bowl, immense harmony is created. The days when I do these space purification rituals, everyone moves around the home with a smile.

Space purifying with the singing bowl

◉ Start by placing the bowl on your left palm on the small cushion and walk slowly from room to room in your home. Strike the bowl three times with the mallet each time you enter a room and move in a clockwise direction around each of the rooms. For purposes of space purification, you need to aim for a continuous, clear or humming sound as you move with the bowl from room to room and from door to door. Striking the rim of the bowl three times creates the first set of sounds. Let the sound ring out loud and follow its resonance. As the sound begins to fade, strike again, and keep doing this as you move around the room.

◉ Another way to set the tones in the bowl ringing is to rub the mallet around the rim of the bowl in a clockwise direction. Keep a firm tension on the mallet and listen as a gentle humming sound grows in intensity. If you cannot get the bowl to sing, first try striking the bowl to wake it up and then start rubbing

This is one of the best ways of holding the singing bowl but do what suits you.

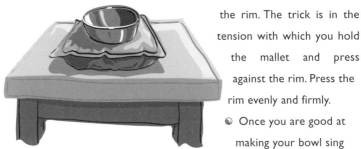

the rim. The trick is in the tension with which you hold the mallet and press against the rim. Press the rim evenly and firmly.

When placed on a cushion the sound of the bowl is considerably enhanced.

🌀 Once you are good at making your bowl sing the sheer beauty of the sound will carry you away as you hear the harmonics. When your bowl is singing nicely, start moving slowly around the rooms of your home and listen to the sounds that are issuing from it. The sound's in dead corners will often be flat and dull while those in a lively part of the home will tend to be sharper and clearer. Learn to tell the difference.

🌀 Stay close to the walls of each room so that any unbalanced energy that is stuck to the walls will be distilled and refined by the sheer purity of the sound. At doors and windows, circle the bowl three times to reinforce the purification process.

🌀 The first time you carry your bowl around your home in this way, you will hear it resonating throughout each room. It will balance the energies almost instantly.

🌀 If you have a room that you consider to be especially unlucky, place the bowl on a table with the cushion

underneath. Let the bowl steady itself and then strike
the rim of the bowl with the wooden mallet.

◉ For enhanced purification, simultaneously chant
mantras, as discussed on pages 41–43.

Adding water to the bowl

For variety of practice you might wish to put some water
into the bowl. Begin with a small amount of water and
gradually add more. Try rubbing the bowl with the mallet
and see if you like the sound created. Keep adding water
until you discover a tone that you like. It is only by
experimenting that you will be able to find the sound that
has an affinity with both you and your space. If you cannot
get a nice sound that you like, use the striking method.

There are some masters who are so good at using water
and sounds to purify the energies of the home that by half
filling a bowl with water and then striking it with a mallet,
they can create a fountain in the bowl. These fountains rise
up and even create a star shape in the water.
This is believed to create a great deal
of auspicious energy. Water fountain
purification like this is excellent for
purifying the energies of the
home just before important
happy occasions like marriages
and birthdays.

Create a different sound by adding water to your singing bowl.

A f t e r w o r d

Space clearing and purifying complement the
practice of feng shui. The rituals are not necessarily
part of the science of feng shui itself. The space
clearing and purification practices described here
may seem esoteric and suggest connotations of
spirituality, but they do not change the essence of
feng shui practice. They do not make feng shui a
spiritual or religious practice.

For centuries, space clearing and purification had been the
exclusive domain of master practitioners of the esoteric.
Monks and professional Taoist magicians would clear and
purify the homes of the rich and powerful based on special
knowledge of rituals and special chanting – all for a fee or
donation. In so doing, they would use the most exotic
scents and aromas expressly brewed or prepared from
herbs taken from holy mountains. In China, there is a big
mountain known as Paradise Mountain where it was
believed grew the fruits and plants of immortality. Thus
were space purifying rituals complemented with specially
prepared ingredients.

Even today, in places like Hong Kong, Taiwan, Singapore and Malaysia, the wealthy arrange for annual house cleansing rituals to ensure that crisp new energy pervades their household through the rest of the year. Homes are also cleared and purified after a death in the family, especially a death that follows a long illness of the family patriarch. And definitely special rituals always accompany the occupancy of a new home. So although feng shui is a separate practice, space purifying has always been regarded as a necessary complement. The luck of any space is enhanced when it has been correctly feng shui-ed; but it feels even better when the energy in the space has been purified.

It is important to remember that feng shui takes care only of 33 per cent of our luck. This is based on the trinity of luck where the other two components of luck are heaven luck (fate or karma) and mankind luck (that which we create for ourselves). We can complement the practice of feng shui by using other means to take care of the remaining 66 per cent of our luck. Use space purification to strongly enhance mankind luck and chant holy mantras to enhance heaven luck.

In the use of feng shui, as in the practice of everything – even science – there is always room for the creative, the esoteric, the spiritual. Furthermore, spirituality is an integral part of our lives, whether we like it or not. The potency of things esoteric or spiritual should not be ignored. My way of embracing spirituality is through my practice of feng shui. In so doing, I do not regard feng shui as either a religion or a spiritual practice but I combine my knowledge of space enhancing rituals with that of feng shui. In this way, I have found the practice of feng shui to be spectacularly successful.

Thus I share these wonderful practices with you and hope they bring you great happiness and a lighter load, the way they have done for me.

Further reading

Too, Lillian *Basic Feng Shui,*
Konsep Books,
Kuala Lumpur, 1997

Too, Lillian *Chinese Astrology
for Romance & Relationships,*
Konsep Books,
Kuala Lumpur, 1996

Too, Lillian, *Chinese Numerology
in Feng Shui,* Konsep Books,
Kuala Lumpur, 1994

Too, Lillian *The Complete
Illustrated Guide to Feng Shui,*
Element Books,
Shaftesbury, 1996

Too, Lillian *The Complete
Illustrated Guide to Feng Shui
for Gardens,* Element Books,
Shaftesbury, 1998

Too, Lillian *Dragon Magic,*
Konsep Books,
Kuala Lumpur, 1996

Too, Lillian, *Feng Shui,*
Konsep Books,
Kuala Lumpur, 1993

Too, Lillian *Practical
Applications for Feng Shui,*
Konsep Books,
Kuala Lumpur, 1994

Too, Lillian *Water Feng Shui
for Wealth,* Konsep Books,
Kuala Lumpur, 1995

Walters, Derek *Feng Shui
Handbook: A Practical Guide
to Chinese Geomancy and
Environmental Harmony,*
Aquarian Press, 1991

Kwok, Man-Ho and
O'Brien, Joanne
The Elements of Feng Shui,
Element Books,
Shaftesbury, 1991

Skinner, Stephen
*Living Earth Manual
of Feng Shui: Chinese
Geomancy,* Penguin, 1989

About
the author

Lillian Too has become the world's bestselling writer on feng shui. Her books have penetrated every corner of the globe and have been translated into fifteen languages. She has made bestseller lists in nine countries, reaching number one in the UK, USA and Singapore. Her books include: *The Complete Illustrated Guide to Feng Shui*, *The Complete Illustrated Guide to Feng Shui for Gardens*, the *Feng Shui Fundamentals* series of nine books, *Lillian Too's Little Book of Feng Shui* and *Lillian Too's Little Book of Feng Shui at Work*.

Lillian Too is an MBA graduate from the Harvard Business School in Boston, USA. She lives in Malaysia, where she heads her own publishing and investment company. She is described by Malaysia's leading business magazine, *Malaysian Business,* as being "Something of a legend in corporate circles being the first woman there to become the Managing Director of a public listed company." Lillian Too is married with one daughter.

Lillian Too's Website address is:
www.lillian-too.com
Also check out www.worldoffengshui.com
– the first online feng shui magazine.

Index